Wel(

desig|

you p

In a v

that the readings and activities within will
help you find a quiet place where you can
contemplate the festival of Christ's birth.

We recommend that you spread the sections
over the course of Advent as they divide into
five sections, four for the weeks of Advent and
the last for Christmas itself.

Please look at the comments at the back of
this book for some additional thoughts and
ideas.

The Advent
Creative Retreat
ACTIVITY BOOK

With every blessing,

Mary and Mark Fleeson
Holy Island

Hope

In 1886 American clergyman, Henry Van Dyke, wrote a brilliant short fictional story about 'The Other Wise Man'.

...a tall, dark man of about forty years, with brilliant eyes set near together under his broad brow, and firm lines graven around his fine, thin lips; the brow of a dreamer and the mouth of a soldier, a man of sensitive feeling but inflexible will, one of those who, in whatever age they may live, are born for inward conflict and a life of quest.

Artaban was a follower of Zoroaster who, with some of his contemporaries, had discerned that a new King was to be born. He prepared to join his three friends on their pilgrimage to Jerusalem.

"I have made ready for the journey. I have sold my possessions, and bought these three jewels - a sapphire, a ruby, and a pearl - to carry them as tribute to the King."

The Pilgrim sets out to meet the others but before he arrives he comes across a sick man, left to die in the desert. Artaban gives the man food, wine and medicine and stays with him to see him restored a little. The man blesses him and tells him that the child he seeks will be found in Bethlehem.

Sadly Artaban misses the departure of his friends due to the delay and has to return to the nearby city to purchase camels and provisions for his solo journey, the unexpected cost forces him to sell his first gift for the King, the beautiful sapphire.

READ The Other Wise Man by Henry Van Dyke, it is in the public domain and available at:
w w w . g u t e n b e r g . o r g
/ e b o o k s / 1 0 6 7 9

In Van Dyke's story Artaban discusses with his fellow disciples of Zoroaster about the teachings that suggest an endless conflict between light and dark. Artaban is not satisfied with the absence of hope and questions the wisdom of waiting for something that will never happen, he quotes other teachings of his faith which foretell of a victor who *...shall make life everlasting, incorruptible, and immortal, and the dead shall rise again"*

Artaban longed for the arrival of the prophesied hero and he tells his friends that he is going to find him but they don't want their comfortable lives rocked by a foreign Saviour who may take their power away and one by one they make their excuses not to join him on his journey.

During Advent we remember the wait for the Messiah whose birth, life, death and resurrection fulfilled hundreds of prophecies.

We also anticipate the return of Jesus.

**The Christian faith is a hopeful one,
it assures us that we are loved,
that we are worth saving for eternal life.
That no matter how far we stray from being
the ideal human, we are never too far away
to seek God.**

One thing have I asked of the LORD, that will I seek after: that I may dwell in the house of the LORD all the days of my life, to gaze upon the beauty of the LORD and to inquire in his temple. For he will hide me in his shelter in the day of trouble; he will conceal me under the cover of his tent; he will lift me high upon a rock. Psalm 27:4-5

Follow the two interwoven knots on this page with your finger.

As you trace the first knot think about what it means to hope for something wonderful, is it a vain wish or, like it says in the dictionary, an 'expectation of the fulfilment of a promise. Trust.'

As you follow the second knot think about where you have been led so far, have you been following God?

Will you continue to follow?

Prepare

Any event or celebration needs preparation, if you're going to celebrate Jesus' birth then you'll probably find yourself preparing by buying or making gifts, Carol singing and decorating your home but it can be useful to think a little more deeply about the season.

The early church recognised the human need to celebrate together so they replaced the much anticipated and enjoyed pagan festivals with ones that had a Christ-centred focus, it's very unlikely that Jesus was born in the midwinter!

Preparation during Advent traditionally is a time of repentance (mind), fasting (body) and prayer (spirit) so that our whole selves are humbled, cleansed and ready to greet the King.

Let's explore each aspect...

MIND
Repentance
noun
/rɪˈpɛnt(ə)ns/
'sincere regret or remorse'

What are you sorry for?

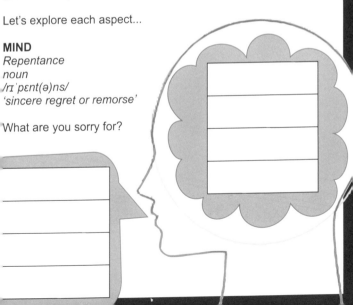

BODY
Fast
verb
/fɑːst/
'abstain from all or some kinds of food or drink'

As you reach for another mince pie you may feel that there could be more to the Christmas season than overindulging! Strict fasting isn't for everyone but consider what else you could give up or, as an alternative, what you could do as a sacrificial practice, i.e. you could give up sweets and/or light a candle each day and pray for someone you know. Spend some time asking God if there is anything that He wants you to give up or to do.

SPIRIT
Prayer
noun
/prɛː/
'a request for help or expression of thanks addressed to God'

David Adam, the well known author, once said that he wrote a prayer every day as a spiritual discipline. Try the idea for yourself, set your own guidelines, maybe just thirty words or four lines. Write them down and ponder them for a while, make a note of anything more that God reveals to you during that time and enter into it with the expectation that more WILL be revealed.
OR
Set aside a few minutes each day to say the prayer below.

Show me Your ways, teach me Your paths,
Grant me the courage to follow You wherever You lead,
The faith to seek You in all things, all places, all people,
And the wisdom to accept that I need You.

SHOW ME YOUR WAYS LORD TEACH ME YOUR PATHS

Joy

Originally Advent was treated similarly to Lent, it was a time for fasting and repentance. The middle Sunday of Advent, like the middle Sunday of Lent, traditionally allowed a break from the fasting and an opportunity to look forward with joy to Jesus' arrival. It may also be known as Gaudete (Rejoice) Sunday.

It's alright to be joyful!

Sometimes I find it hard to reconcile happenings in the world with a loving, caring God and sometimes it's hard to raise a smile let alone a joyful spirit.

Sometimes I feel guilty for enjoying something when I know that there are people suffering and I'm not doing anything about it. I have to very deliberately remind myself that getting down about the bad things isn't going to make them go away, instead I have to seek God in the ordinary and be ready to do God's will in all things, be ready to speak out for the oppressed, feed the hungry, visit the sick and imprisoned when I'm given the opportunity and when I am prompted by the Spirit to do so.

Sometimes I have to accept that I can't do everything, my calling at this time is to prioritise the family and work God has given me. I can't do what Joe does and it would be wrong to try.

Sometimes I have to force myself to smile and laugh and find the good in the world - and that's alright too.

Ring forth, ye bells, with clarion sound - Forget your knells, for joys abound. Forget your notes of mournful lay, And from your throats pour joy to-day.

Words from the opening chorus of 'The Sorceror' by Gilbert and Sullivan and 'Blessed be the Name of my Rock' by Chuck Gerard

Blow the trumpet in Zion, for I am coming soon

Gaudete, gaudete!
Christus est natus
Ex Maria virgine, gaudete!
Tempus adest grati
Hoc quod optabamus,
Carmina l titi
Devote reddamus.
Deus homo factus est
Natura mirante,
Mundus renovatus est
A Christo regnante.
Ezechielis porta
Clausa pertransitur,
Unde lux est orta
Salus invenitur.
Ergo nostra contio
Psallat iam in lustro;
Benedicat Domino:
Salus Regi nostro.

Rejoice, rejoice! Christ is born
Of the Virgin Mary, rejoice!
The time of grace has come,
    what we have wished for,
        songs of joy
Let us give back faithfully.
God has become man,
To the wonderment of Nature,
The world has been renewed
    By the reigning Christ.
The closed gate of Ezekiel
    Is passed through,
Whence the light is born,
    Salvation is found.
Therefore let our gathering
    Now sing in brightness
Let it give praise to the Lord;
    Greeting to our King.

Artaban moved steadily on
until he arrived at Bethlehem. A
was the third day after the three Wi
Men had come to that place and ha
found Mary and Joseph, with the
young child, Jesus, and had laid their
gifts of gold and frankincense and
myrrh at his feet.

"But the travellers disappeared again," she
continued, "as suddenly as they had come.
We were afraid at the strangeness of their
visit. We could not understand it. The man
of Nazareth took the child and his mother,
and fled away that same night secretly, and
it was whispered that they were going to
Egypt."

Artaban missed the baby Jesus and
instead found himself in the midst of
Herod's order to kill all the male babies.
When the soldiers arrive at the door of his
host, who had a new born child, he says to
them that there is no child in the house and
bribes the captain to leave.

"I am all alone in this place, and I am waiting
to give this jewel to the prudent captain who
will leave me in peace."

He showed the ruby,
glistening in the
hollow of his hand like
a great drop of blood.

His remorse is
heartbreaking, he
has lied and given
another of his
precious gifts away
but he saved the life
of an innocent child.

In the late seventies a popular song listed 'Reasons to be Cheerful' it had a catchy tune and taught a simple lesson in counting your blessings.

Write a list of ten things that make you feel joyful today...

1
2
3
4
5
6
7
8
9
10

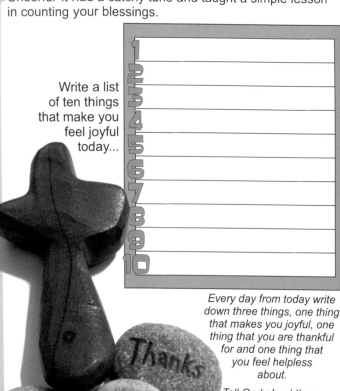

Every day from today write down three things, one thing that makes you joyful, one thing that you are thankful for and one thing that you feel helpless about.

Tell God about them.

It may help to have three pebbles and a small cross, as you think of the things place them at the foot of the cross.

Thanks

Help

Love

What is Love?

Follow the spiral to the centre with your finger and think about what love means to you personally then from the centre say the words from Corinthians as you return to the start.

LOVE ALWAYS PROTECTS. LOVE ALWAYS TRUSTS. LOVE ALWAYS HOPES. LOVE ALWAYS PERSEVERES. LOVE DOES NOT DELIGHT IN EVIL. LOVE REJOICES WITH THE TRUTH. LOVE IS NOT EASILY ANGERED. LOVE KEEPS NO RECORD OF WRONGS. LOVE DOES NOT DISHONOUR OTHERS. LOVE IS NOT SELF-SEEKING. LOVE IS NOT PROUD. LOVE DOES NOT BOAST. LOVE DOES NOT ENVY. LOVE IS PATIENT. LOVE IS KIND.

For God so loved the world that he gave his only begotten Son, that whosoever believeth in him should not perish, but have everlasting life.
John 3:16

Jesus teach me how to love, how to live in Your presence.
Jesus teach me how to live, how to pray in Your will.
Jesus teach me how to pray, how to rest in Your embrace.
Jesus teach me how to rest, how to be in Your world.
Jesus teach me how to be, how to love in Your way.

And there were in the same country shepherds in the field, keeping watch over their flock by night.

And the angel of the Lord came to them, and the glory of the Lord shone around them, and they were very afraid.

And the angel said to them, **"Fear not, for I bring you good news of great joy,** which shall be to all people.

For to you is born this day in the City of David **a Saviour, who is Christ the Lord.** And this shall be a sign to you: You shall find the Baby wrapped in swaddling clothes, lying in a manger."

And suddenly there was with the angel a multitude of the heavenly host praising God and saying,

"Glory to God in the highest, and on earth peace, good will!"

And it came to pass, when the angels were gone away from them, the shepherds said one to another, "Let us now go now to Bethlehem and see this thing that has come to pass, which the Lord has made known unto us."

And they came with haste and found Mary and Joseph, and the Baby lying in a manger.

One of the greatest expressions of love has to be trust, complete faith in someone, the story of Jesus' birth is full of moments of total trust, Mary trusted God; the Shepherds trusted the angels; the Wise Men trusted God when he spoke in their dreams; Joseph trusted God.

Imagine how the story might have ended prematurely if Joseph hadn't trusted God's Messenger and had stayed in Bethlehem!

Jesus commanded his disciples, and therefore us, to love one another in the same way as he loved them and us. Jesus' love is the same love that God showed for the world in sending his Son and so in giving that command Jesus is showing that he has great trust in our capacity for love, he knows that we are capable of immense love. We were created to love!

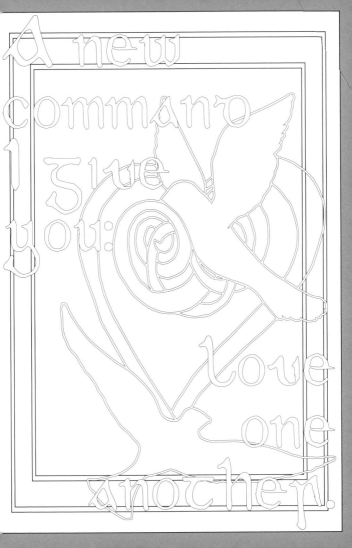

Light

On Christmas Day take a few minutes to consider what it means to be a light in the world.

Can we hide away if we are meant to be a light?

Can we be broken and still shine?

What is the light? Is it goodness? Is it faith? Is it the Holy Spirit? Is it you? Is it life itself?

How can you deliberately be a light to others?

Jesus said, "I am the light of the world. Whoever follows me will never walk in darkness, but will have the light of life."

John 8:12 (NIV)

FOLLOW HIM

"The mug was broken but we placed a torch inside and realised that the light could be seen, brightly shining through the hole. Isn't life a bit like that?"
(Taize International Meeting, Budapest 1992)